Muslim Scientists

IBN MAJID
The Master Navigator

Published by Ali Gator Productions
Copyright © 2021 Ali Gator Productions, Second Edition,
First Published 2017

National Library of Australia Cataloguing–in-Publication (CIP) data:
Ahmed Imam
ISBN: 978-1-921772-40-5
For primary school age, Juvenile fiction, Dewey Number: 823.92

Adapted from the original title Ilmuan Muslim Ibnu Majid first published by Pelangi Mizan.
Copyright © 2015 by Author Risma Dewi, Illustrator Nano. Printed in Indonesia.

ALi GATOR

T: +61 (3) 9386 2771
P.O. Box 2536, Regent West, Melbourne Victoria, 3072 Australia
E: info@ali-gator.com W: www.ali-gator.com

بِسْمِ اللهِ الرَّحْمٰنِ الرَّحِيْمِ

BISMILLAHIR RAHMANIR RAHIM
IN THE NAME OF ALLAH, MOST GRACIOUS, MOST MERCIFUL

Inspiring our children to learn about
the great Muslim scientists, scholars
and adventurers from
the Golden Age of Islam.

NOTES TO PARENTS AND TEACHERS

The Muslim Scientists Series aims to introduce to young readers some of the famous Muslim scientists, scholars and adventurers who discovered and invented many things that we use today and take for granted.

It is our hope that young children will be inspired by these amazing people and be encouraged to pursue their own path of discovery and questioning. It all starts with a passion for learning.

Whilst reading about Ibn Majid, "The Master Navigator", discuss with the children about how excited Ibn Majid must have been as a young boy to go on his first adventure out on the open seas.

Ask the children if they have ever been on a boat and what was that like ? Or have they ever used a compass, or know what a compass is ? Or how a compass helps us know which way to pray as Muslims ?

In Sha Allah (God Willing) if this series helps to inspire our young readers to be the next generation of thinkers, to better mankind through inventions and discoveries, then we have truly met our goal.

This is Ahmad ibn Majid,
but everyone calls him Ibn Majid.

He was born into a famous family of sailors,
in a small seaside town in Oman, in 1432.

As a young boy Ibn Majid heard
many stories from his family about
the lands beyond the Red Sea
and the Indian Ocean.
Ibn Majid so wanted to be
a sailor like his father.

One day Ibn Majid's father gave him
some advice, "Memorize the Qur'an,
read books about sea travel and
learn what's in them by heart
and In Sha Allah you can join
me on my travels."

6

Ibn Majid studied very hard and learned everything that his father had asked.

He was now ready to embark on his maiden voyage.

Ibn Majid was so excited. He steered the ship a little, but his main role was to man the rudder at the back to guide the ship along, and to take measurements along the journey.

Through the blessings of Allah, Ibn Majid became
very knowledgeable about all the roles on a ship.

Yet his real expertise was as a Navigator, making sure that
the ship followed its course, to reach its destination safely.

Ibn Majid helped many people travel across the open seas,
following maps and discovering new places.

Ibn Majid is famous for helping
the Portuguese explorer Vasco da Gama.

Together they discovered new sailing
routes from Europe to India using maps
that only the Arabs had at that time.

Because Ibn Majid visited so many countries, he could speak many languages, Arabic, Persian, Tamil and East African.

People started to call him "The Lion of the Sea".

His family was very happy that he had carried on the family tradition.

Alhamdulillah.

ALHAMDULILLAH - PRAISE BE TO ALLAH

One day Ibn Majid decided to put a magnetic needle into a box, and created what today is known as a Compass.

This allowed Ibn Majid and other sailors to always know where North was to guide their ships.

When you are out on the open seas and the wind is blowing, it can be very easy to get lost.

Ibn Majid would use his compass to measure where he was, to help him reach his destination safely.

After many years at sea Ibn Majid wrote a great book about everything he had learned about navigation. It is known as a "Navigation Encyclopedia" and can be found today at the French National Library in Paris.

Ibn Majid had truly mastered the world of navigation and shipping.

21

Even with his compass, Ibn Majid always remembered
that all his journeys could only be achieved by
having Tawakal – Trust in Allah.

That it was only Allah who would protect him
and guide him when he was far out
in the open sea.

23

DUA' FOR PUTTING YOUR TRUST IN ALLAH

The Prophet Muhammad (PBUH) encouraged us
every time we leave our house,
to say the following* :

بِسْمِ اللّهِ تَوَكَّلْتُ عَلَى اللّهِ، لَا حَوْلَ وَلَا قُوَّةَ إِلَّا بِاللّهِ

Bismillahi Tawakaltu `Aala Allahi,
La Hawla wa La Kuwata, illa Billah.

"In the Name of Allah, I trust Allah;
there is no might and no Power, but with Allah."

* Sunan Abu Dawud

PBUH – PEACE BE UPON HIM